PLATO

&

MODERN EDUCATION

PLATO
&
MODERN EDUCATION

BY

SIR RICHARD LIVINGSTONE

THE REDE LECTURE
1944

CAMBRIDGE: AT THE UNIVERSITY PRESS

NEW YORK: THE MACMILLAN COMPANY

1944

PLATO & MODERN EDUCATION

FOR MORE THAN 2000 years education has been with us, a vital interest, a continual problem; much has been written about it, but little of enduring value. The great books on it could be counted on the fingers of two hands—perhaps, if we judge strictly, of one—and among them two date from before the birth of Christ. Possibly Aristotle should not be included among these, but the few pages at the close of the *Politics* are pure gold and suggest that what is lost must be among the missing works of antiquity most worth recovering. With Plato, we have been more fortunate. He wrote no single work on the subject, but it engaged his mind from the first, and five of the dialogues belonging to his earlier period contain passages dealing with it, though his great pronouncements are in the *Republic* and the *Laws*.

In politics, profound as is Plato's thought, his actual prescriptions are of little practical use to us. The *Republic* raises question after question, but, as its author himself says, the commonwealth which he proposes belongs to heaven rather than to earth; and the constitution in the *Laws*, designed for a city community isolated from its neighbours, might be tried as an experiment, if Ulster or Eire could be transplanted to the solitudes of the mid-Pacific, but would hardly work even there and is certainly impracticable in a world of great states. Plato is more often a master of diagnosis than of cure; if he did not solve a problem, he always knew what it was. That is not faint praise, for in political and social questions true diagnosis is the first need and the rarest gift. But in education Plato is more than a diagnostician. Most of his suggestions are perfectly practical, and illustrate that uncanny power of divining what was yet unborn, which no other writer, ancient or modern, possesses so highly, and which makes him so often seem more modern than ourselves. How often he has anticipated reforms wholly alien to the society of his own time, of which some were not accepted till many centuries later, some are still to come! Here are a few examples. Plato held that women and men were to receive the same education:[1] it is an amazing notion for a society where women were inferior beings confined to the home, and one that had to wait for the late nineteenth century before slowly and painfully it won acceptance. He declared that education must be compulsory for every child: in 1876 this country came to the same conclusion. He declared that the Minister of Education is 'far the most important of the great offices of the state' and that he would be the 'busiest of our officials', and suggested that he should associate with himself suitable citizens of either sex. There you have a Board of Education. Our own (but, unlike Plato's, without women members) did not come into being till 1900, and when I wrote this lecture its President had not yet become a Minister. Or turn from administration to methods. Plato divined the importance of pre-natal

[1] *Laws*, 813.

6

influences on the unborn child and the significance for character-forming of the first three years of life—'no inconsiderable time', he says, 'to be spent ill or well'. He directed that 'all children, from three to six, shall be collected at the local sanctuary—all the children of each village being assembled at the same place' in the charge of nurses controlled by a superintendent, not to learn lessons but to lead an ordered life: 'nature herself suggests games at that age, and children readily invent them when left in each other's company.' There you have the modern nursery school. At the other end of life Plato is the parent of adult education. He did not hold the strange view, which we are beginning to abandon, that education could be completed at school or at university: his ruling class only reach the climax of their education at 50, and even then continue to divide their lives between action and thought, the world and the study.[1] In all this Plato shows a penetrating insight into the practice as well as the theory of education.

But there is another reason why his views on it should be interesting to us. His age had to face the same problem as our own, and he realised its gravity, whilst we are still almost unaware of it. He was born into a world which, with all its dissimilarities from the twentieth century, resembles it in one very important point. It was an age of reason, as no age has been between the second and nineteenth centuries of our era: the modern temper has never been better expressed than in the words of Heraclitus: 'The highest excellence is Thought: and Wisdom consists in

[1] Ib. 804, 765, 792, 794, 813; *Republic*, 540.

saying the truth, and acting according to Nature, listening to her.[1] The acceptance of this momentous principle led in fifth-century Greece as in modern Europe to the shattering of traditional views not only on nature but also on religion, morals and politics. That age had to face the questions which, now veiled now visible, now remote now insistent, constitute the eternal human problem—what should men believe about life, how should they live it, in what state of society can the good life be best lived, how can we create such a state? These questions haunted Plato in early life and occupied his mature thought, and he had to answer them not by appeal to tradition or to revelation, but by the unaided reason. They are the very questions which we ought to be facing at this moment; they have been forced on us by the cause which forced them on Plato— the impact of reason on accepted traditions and beliefs; they must be answered by the light of reason; and now as then they make apparent a task of education, sometimes overlooked in ages of comfort or of rigid convention.

Early in life when he wrote the *Euthydemus* Plato gave his view of the ultimate purpose of education in words that might have been written as a warning to us. All men, he says, desire happiness. Health, beauty, good birth, wealth, power, honour are ingredients in it. But in themselves these are neutral; they are good or bad according to the use made of them; they can be, and often are, misused; indeed, if a man does not know how to use them, he is better without them, for they are opportunities for evil, ministers, as

[1] Fr. 112.

8

Plato says, to the evil principle which then may control them.[1] That clearly is true not only of the goods which Plato mentions but of all that men possess or desire, of knowledge and intellect, freedom and peace. Their value depends on our having the wisdom that can employ them rightly. This then must be the final aim of education, which is defined as 'training to goodness from youth'.[2] It is needed by the individual. 'Children', as Plato says, 'are a man's riches, the greatest of his possessions, and the whole fortune of his house depends on whether they turn out ill or well.'[3] It is necessary to the state. 'So long as the young generation is, and continues to be, well brought-up, our ship of state will have a fair voyage; otherwise the consequences are better left unspoken.'[4] Thus the teacher's task is given. He must create 'the virtue, which is the master of all virtues—wisdom and reason and right conviction, with the passionate longing which attends them'.[5] He must get rid of ignorance, and 'the greatest ignorance is when men do not love but hate what reason shows to be right'. To this end all education is bent, and every instrument in it used. When the child goes to school, 'the works of great poets are put into his hands, and he learns them by heart',[6] that he may see what human greatness is and desire to imitate it. He learns music that it may mould his soul to rhythm and harmony. In his later education mathematics are used, not for any immediate

[1] 281.   [2] *Laws*, 643.
[3] *Laches*, 185.   [4] *Laws*, 813.   [5] Ib. 688 f.
[6] *Protagoras*, 326 f.; *Republic*, 522 f., 526, 529 f., 410 f.

9

practical end but to accustom his mind, through their abstract forms, to look past the flux of changing phenomena to the incorporeal, eternal world of being; he studies Harmonics and Astronomy so that as he contemplates the stars,

'Which are the brain of heaven...'

he may be imbued with a sense of the beauty of order and law. Games and physical training are not merely necessary to health and development of the body but to balance and correct intellectual pursuits.[1] The mere athlete is brutal or philistine; the mere intellectual is either unstable or else over-civilised and spiritless; and the right education must tune the two strings of body and mind to a perfect spiritual harmony. And as every subject in education plays its part in moulding the human being, so do the surroundings in which they are studied. The most famous passage on education in Plato is the one in which he insists on the importance of atmosphere in education: 'the young should live in a wholesome climate and drink in good from every quarter, so that like a wind bringing health from healthy lands, some influence from noble works may from childhood upward constantly fall on ear and eye and insensibly draw them into sympathy and harmony with the beauty of reason.'[2]

I have no time to speak of Plato's views on the importance of indirect influences, of atmosphere, in education; they deserve a study to themselves. Here he has seen far deeper than we yet do. How little we have appreciated

[1] *Republic*, 410 f.   [2] Ib. 401.

10

even the elements of the problem, can be seen by considering the conditions in which the majority of English children grow up. In Oxford and Cambridge, in Winchester and Eton and elsewhere, we or our ancestors have done what Plato wished and created places where the winds bring 'health from healthy lands'; but most English education takes place in very different surroundings. If the makers of nineteenth-century England had read and understood Plato, they would have built most of their schools very differently, nor would so many newer universities have started life with architectural millstones hung round their necks.

Even vocational studies are viewed by Plato in their relation to character. He recognises their necessity, and his youth learn arithmetic for its use in business, geometry for war, astronomy for agriculture and navigation. Yet, though he draws a clear line between them and liberal education, he sees, with characteristic acuteness, that such studies have a liberal element and affect character. The *Laches* begins with a discussion of training in the use of arms. Here is a question of a single field of education, a narrowly technical subject—ought or ought not the young to learn how to fight in heavy armour? But behind and beneath it lies something deeper. The end of this knowledge is more than success on the battle-field: it is 'the soul of the young'.[1] Military studies have their specific object, but also a wider aim and result, for education is not a mere congeries of subjects; it is, whether you intend it or not,

[1] 185.

a whole whose parts all ultimately converge on and influence the soul.

In fine, for Plato the supreme aim of education is human goodness, but goodness of a far wider kind than our normal use of the word suggests. Conduct in the narrower sense is only a part of the natural habit of a mind attuned to ultimate reality, 'intimate with the eternal order of things and the music of the spheres'. Nothing matters compared with this. For, as Plato says, the ignorance most fatal to states and individuals is not ignorance in the field of technology or of the professions, but spiritual ignorance.[1] So he conceives education essentially as a training in values. This seems to me the most important truth that we can learn from Plato.

There was a time when we knew it, when English education was Platonic in this sense. To Milton its aim was 'to know God aright and out of that knowledge to love him, to imitate him, to be like him, by possessing our souls of true virtue'; Thomas Arnold defined it as

'teaching our understandings to know the highest truth, teaching our affections to love the highest good.... The great work of education is to make us love what is good, and therefore not only know it but do it.'[2]

Milton and Arnold agreed with Plato's definition of education as 'training to goodness'. We could hardly claim that this spirit guided and informed modern education. It is

[1] Laws, 689.

[2] Milton, Tractate on Education; Arnold, Sermon on Education and Instruction (Jan. 24, 1841).

sporadically present there; the moralistic bent of British character stresses conduct; the deep influence of Christianity on the nation still colours our purposes; Arnold created a tradition which has profoundly influenced higher education; in the older universities College Chapels and Chaplains are at least a symbol of a life ruled by spiritual ends. But we could hardly claim that our aim is Plato's: and indeed when we look for an aim, it is difficult to discern. Our eyes are blinded by a dust-storm of School Certificates, Higher Certificates, Scholarships, Degrees, Diplomas, Examinations beyond counting; the air is full of the loud demands of industry, commerce and the professions, and through the din and mist the figure of education is faintly descried. On closer view, she seems more like Proteus than Athene, and mainly occupied with other interests than the training of the soul which Plato thought her true business. Why has she lost the clear and earnest purpose of earlier days?

One answer is that she is living not among Greeks but among the English. Theory is not our strong point; how many schools or teachers are haunted by an overmastering purpose beyond the business of the hour? We go about education in the English fashion, meeting immediate needs, feeling our way, unguided by any very exact aim; like some low, though efficient, type of organism, which adapts itself subconsciously to its immediate surroundings. The Greeks were different, not instinctive but rational, following the argument where it leads, undeterred by prejudice, unobstructed by compromise. Pure thought brought them out of barbarism to civilisation, out of superstition to rational religious and moral systems. Pure thought led Democritus to argue that the universe was constructed of atoms in infinite space. Pure thought led Plato in a wholly unfeminist world to say that women could and should engage in all the activities of men, and in a society based on slave labour led a writer of the fifth century B.C. to say 'God left all men free: nature has made no man a slave'.[1] This is prophecy, though not after the manner of Isaiah or Amos: the voice that here speaks through human lips is that of reason. This unfettered activity of the mind makes the Greeks still incomparable guides to life, not only because of their sane and noble view of it, but because they are the great exemplars of the temper in which its problems should be faced. They had an instinct for exact definition, and, in life as in literature, for that unity of design which is the mark of the artist, and the essence of a work of art. 'Every art', Aristotle's *Ethics* begin, 'every inquiry, every action and undertaking seems to aim at some good.' Yes; but not perhaps all English 'actions and undertakings'. It is unfortunate if we have less natural clear-sightedness than the Greeks, for, living in a world infinitely more complicated than theirs, we need it more.

One difference between that world and our own is that there are no words in Greek for Board of Education, Local Education Authority, examination, or indeed for most topics which fill the pages of educational papers and absorb the attention of educational conferences. Plato was neither

[1] Alcidamas: see on Aristotle, *Rhet.* 1373 b 18.

14

country it has been felt only in mild and fitful airs. Th[e] forces which have disturbed our course are different permanent and universal. The whole world is subject t[o] them and they will increase rather than lessen. Sinc[e] Plato's day, three new influences have affected educatio[n] all legitimate but each tending to obscure its aim as he co[n] ceived it; the accumulation of knowledge, the need [of] earning a living, the growth of applied science. Let m[e] briefly review these in turn.

Greek civilisation was one of thought and life rath[er] than things. It possessed and needed so much less know[ ]ledge than our own, it had not to master the accumulatio[n] of the two last millennia of human activity, and therefo[re] was never tempted to confuse education with learning [or] information. Most of the subjects which fill our text-book[s] and school time-tables did not exist or existed only in rudimentary form. There were no foreign languages t[o] master—did any Greek learn even Persian or Egyptian[?] What we call 'the knowledge that an educated man shoul[d] possess' was a light burden for a Greek boy, and he was le[ss] occupied than the modern child in painfully acquiring i[n] formation and quickly losing it. He started on the journe[y] of life with a small handbag of knowledge where we r[e] quire several heavy Saratoga trunks. In such a time it w[as] easy for education to have a clear and undivided aim.

Nor had it to train men to make a living. The thinke[rs] and writers of ancient Greece belonged to a class of happ[y] *rentiers* who knew how to use that privilege and were n[ot] obsessed by the need of earning their bread: this object [ ]

helped nor hampered by an educational system. All systems once established tend to cease thinking, except intermittently, and operate by their own momentum; and here educational systems are no better than Churches or States or Social Orders. The machine once started functions as an end in itself, and, self-content, forgets the purposes for which it was created. The Greek world was not one of machinery, and a particular form of it, which we spend much time in operating, did not exist; no examination distracted teacher and pupil from the true aims of education to processes which at their best may be parallel to it but in fact are often widely divergent. We suffer from these dis- tractions. That is one reason why our educational purpose in practice, if not in theory, is less clear than Plato's. There are ages when intelligent improvisation may do the work of a clearly conceived purpose. Ours is not one of them. Without a clear aim we are jostled and confused by its complications, and our social structures become a medley of ill-assorted adaptations to successive needs. No pilot sets the ship's course and it drifts before the prevailing wind. That has been our fate. Consider some of the winds that have driven our ship out of its course.

One wind that has affected our ship, and influenced both our theory and our practice, blows from Rousseau. Among the great modern improvements in education is the attempt to start from the angle of the child and plan education ac- cording to his nature and capacities. Rabelais, Montaigne, Comenius divined this principle; it was Rousseau, under a flag inscribed with the magic words Nature and Liberty, whose genius, eloquence and passionate exaggeration gave a new direction to education. In the present century psychology, and in America pragmatism, have reinforced his intuitions.

No one can quarrel with the main principles of this movement. The child must be active, not passive. Education is to be a process of living, not a preparation for it. The school is a place, not for giving a body of authoritative information but for developing the child's creative power. Teaching must not outrun his experience or attempt to plant in him knowledge which has no roots in his own. Literary study is to be reduced or even abolished. 'No book other than the world: no instruction other than facts. The child who reads does not think, he only reads: he is not instructed, he learns words.'[1]

Rousseau's phrases do indeed remind us of a weakness which often besets education, but in them we also detect a danger of which he was unaware. It is true that, intent on what we consider the supreme aim of education, we are all apt to forget the child. But there are two terms in education—the human being and the goal, the child as he is and the child as he should be when his education is done. A theory of education which starts from the aim of education may ignore the learner; a theory which starts from the child may lose sight of the aim. Both must be remembered and reconciled. 'The only true education', writes Professor Dewey, 'comes through the stimulation of the child's

[1] *Émile*, Book 3, p. 179 (edn. Garnier).

powers by the demands of the social situat finds himself.'[1] If we listen to this subt doctrine we must rewrite the ancient text beginning was, not the Word, but the Sit disastrous creed. If it is followed, the child be any better than the society of his time. doubt should be formed by contact with the it must be the right world, not merely the wo day; it must be the world at its best, a wo society as it is, but far higher and better. The of this—if knowledge is the right word—must be it is fatal to forget this term or to misconceive it is not enough to interest the child and make receptive and awake. An active intellectual di important, but even more so is the quality of and this must therefore be carefully chosen. The po the agnosticism, of our age is reflected in its educat fatal results. At the worst it adopts the philoso Micawber and acts on the delusion that child nat to itself will automatically unfold into goodness. commonly it is arbitrarily selective, adopting as i some catchword of the hour and place which the opinion of the moment approves and exempts criticism. Education dissolves into 'projects', and ch more likely to be its result than virtue.

The wind of Rousseau has blown strongly in Amer where its results are not encouraging; in our conservat

[1] *Education To-day*, p. 3.

education never entered their minds. They had enough money to live in simple comfort, not enough to complicate their existence. It is the kind of life which scholars may hope to find in heaven, and to some extent it is lived in universities by professors who have enough teaching to stimulate and keep them human, not enough to distract them from the fascinating pursuit of knowledge. But to be able so to live without distraction from youth to old age—how rarely to-day is this the privilege of those who wish and are fit to use it! Greek thinkers, unlike most of us, were exempt from the sentence, 'In the sweat of thy brow shalt thou eat thy bread.' But we are not exempt and must be equipped to earn a living. Cut out of our education all that is introduced into it specifically for that purpose, and how much simpler its problems would at once become! Vocational training imparts into education a new object which may be consistent with its ultimate purpose but also may have little relevance to it. There is at least a risk of indecision and confusion.

Another source of confusion is the development of science and technology. Science profoundly affected Greek thought but did not alter the conditions of Greek life, and we have the spectacle, so strange to us, of men profoundly interested in it, but almost unaware of its practical uses. To the Athenian thinker of the late fifth and fourth centuries—a fact curiously overlooked in much classical English education—scientific study was essential to the educated life. To Aristophanes, Socrates seemed occupied in it, when he was not concerned with immoral arguments, with the ἄδικος λόγος; half of Aristotle's writings are on the same subject; and every Greek philosophic system, except Cynicism, had its physics as well as its ethics. As we get glimpses of Athenian life in Plato's *Dialogues* or divine its nature from the contemporary literature, architecture and art, we may wonder whether applied science is as indispensable to the good life as is commonly supposed. But though it may have done as much harm as good to the class of persons who already are comfortably off without it, it has enormously increased their number, and in replacing slaves by machinery it has brought the good life within the reach of the masses. Anyhow, there is no question that it is indispensable to our life and therefore must be provided for in our education. But here is another distracting element, a further risk of confusion and divided aims. The modern man finds it harder to remain

'With powers
Fresh, undiverted to the world without,
Firm to their mark, not spent on other things.'

Here are three winds—the need for knowledge, for science, for daily bread—into whose teeth we cannot sail: we must accommodate our course to them without losing sight of our destination; and in some degree they may help us on our way to it. But clearly they tend to give a special direction to education. Inevitably, and within certain limits rightly, its whole trend is towards knowledge and the power to use it: knowledge of many different kinds, of languages and history and literature, of mathematics and science pure and applied, of economics, politics and psychology, of all the categories through which the human mind attempts to class and interpret phenomena: and with it goes training of the intellect to think accurately and to express thought. These results on the whole please us, and from some of the suggestions for educational reform you might suppose that we had only to provide rather more of the same stuff, throwing in a dash of general knowledge and handicrafts, and our work would be done. Plato would have thought that it was hardly begun. Some of our products would have satisfied him less than they do us. He speaks of men who are 'masters of calculation, highly trained in the finest subtleties and in all that makes for quickness of mind'.[1] We recognise a fair description of a type that we are well content to produce: Plato expressly states that such a training is not a qualification for the government of a state. He had lived in a society of quick and subtle minds and did not think them enough: the ignorance which he dreaded was of a different kind and quite compatible with a high degree of intellectual expertise.

Experts and highly trained intelligence are essential, if the modern world is not to collapse. But civilisation is compounded of two elements: the machine, continually growing more efficient and complicated, and the human being. From this dualism spring the chief human problems: the relation of the individual soul to material civilisation, and its relation to society and to the state. The state may cramp the human soul; material civilisation tends to

[1] Laws, 689.

suffocate it painlessly. The danger of such suffocation is the theme of moralists in every age, but clearly it increases as material civilisation develops and men concentrate on managing and improving the machine or are buried under its products. Two forces can counteract this danger— religion and education. Unfortunately, the more civilisation develops, the less education inclines to serve this purpose. It, too, is enslaved to the machine and, absorbed in training people to work it, makes them still more machine-minded and fosters the very evil that it ought to prevent. It is characteristic of to-day that, when we discuss which subjects should be studied, or which languages should be learnt, the first consideration is nearly always utility; we ask what is most useful for the machine, not what is most likely to make a good human being. Neither Plato nor the Middle Ages would have made that mistake.

At times, the right motto for our education seems to be *Propter vitam vivendi perdere causas*: 'For the sake of livelihood to lose what makes life worth living.' The material in life tends to dominate it. The shadow appears in Bacon's legitimate insistence on the study of nature rather than of words. It deepens as 'things' become increasingly important and in the end threatens to absorb man. Spiritual and moral life is forgotten: wisdom and even judgment recede into the background. An age appears which can use hand and eye, follows its vocations with increased efficiency, masters Nature and subdues her to its will, but, lacking ultimate convictions, misuses its illimitable opportunities, and frees itself from slavery to want only to become the slave of its possessions. Because it has knowledge without clear values and beliefs, it drifts on the tide of the moment, and in political or economic collapse is the ready victim of Hitler or Mussolini or anyone with real beliefs, however pernicious, however absurd.

Lately I received within a fortnight of each other two letters that illustrate my point. The writer of the first was in command of an O.C.T.U., and, later, as President of a War Office Selection Board, had the task of choosing potential officers for training; he says: 'The work entails a private interview with men of all ages, between 18 and 45, drawn from every conceivable school and occupation. Exploring these minds, endeavouring to assess these values, has been a profound education. The deepest impression left on me is the general lack of any vision of greatness or any sound basis on which to form true values.' These words refer to the officer class. The second letter, from a private in the Women's Services, says in a different way the same thing about the rank and file. 'People—I am continually coming up against them—seem to lack a clear belief or any philosophy. It is surprising and courageous how they push along at all; several have said, "What is the point of living?" and, "What are we here for, and how can it have any purpose?" And they say it in no particular despondency of the moment, but because they really have no formed idea.' If there is any truth in such views, it is a grave judgment on our education. Such a temper may be less dangerous in war, which imposes a definite aim on us, if not a philosophy. But it is very dangerous in peace. It was from such a spiritual condition, as much as from economic distress, that National Socialism in Germany sprang.

So far as the mass of the people is concerned we might expect such an outlook. For at 14 or earlier more than 80% of the population have hitherto said a final farewell to education and been left to the chances of a good home or a good employer for any direction in the maze of the world. Such neglect mattered less, while the convictions and conventions of the Victorian age marked a clear path of normal conduct, while, read at home or heard week by week in Church and Chapel, the words of the greatest of all religions challenged conduct and strengthened faith. It matters very much in an age when for the masses cinemagoing has replaced Church-going. This is 'the century of the common man'. What will he make of it? We have not done much to help him.

But it is higher education, not the education of the masses that I have in mind, and I now proceed to consider a branch of it in which my audience has a special interest. Every human institution is capable of improvement, but on the whole universities do their work so well that we should be hurt if someone suggested that they had a very inadequate aim, and failed to equip their students for life. That is what I wish to suggest.

There are three essentials in the education of the modern man. One is training for his life's work; this may be specific but is, in higher education at least, more commonly general, giving a mastery of principles rather than of practice. The second is a sense of the place of science in civilisation (this involves some knowledge of economic history, which science so deeply affects): a man can dispense with this, but without it he will hardly understand the history or possibilities of his own age; to this I would add as a corollary and correction that he will understand them still less if he is ignorant of the other forces in civilisation. Finally—and most important—everyone needs a philosophy of life, a sense of values by which to judge and use the gifts of material civilisation. The perfectly educated man would have a standard, a perception of values, in every province— physical, aesthetic, intellectual, moral; in his profession or occupation; in personal, national and international life. He would know the first-rate in all of them and run no risk of being deceived by the inferior. Further, as far as this is possible, he would have a hierarchy of values, so that lesser did not dominate greater goods. No age needs a sense of the first-rate more than our own. We are individualists; without standards to control it, individualism is apt to reveal itself as eccentricity and to end in chaos. We are free; without standards freedom only gives greater latitude of error. Our possessions and opportunities multiply; without standards we have no idea of their relative value, no principle of choice among them, except the whim of the moment. No doubt the perfectly educated man does not exist and never will exist. But the quality of a civilisation depends on the number of people in it who approximate to this standard, and we should at least set such an ideal before us.

But universities make no provision to teach it. They plan, carefully and thoroughly, the training of the chemist, the engineer, the economist, and the rest, but not the training of the human being. The crown of Plato's education is the vision of the Idea of the Good, 'that which sheds light on all things', so that men may have 'a pattern by which to order the state and their own lives and those of their fellow-men'.[1] The crown of our education is the vision of the Idea of Engineering, or the Idea of Physics, or the Idea of Economics, or the Idea of Exact Scholarship. These Ideas are very important, but they do not exhaust human excellence, they throw a limited light on it, and by themselves they are no substitute for some vision of the Idea of the Good.

You may object that I am using out-of-date language in speaking of the Idea of the Good. Then let me translate it into modern idiom. No doubt many of our ways will astonish posterity. Each generation is amused or appalled by much which its predecessors accepted complacently. But I doubt if anything will amaze the future more than the disappearance, sometimes after the School Certificate, but at latest on entrance into the University, of any general study of religion or philosophy; so that at the age when they are becoming able to think on such subjects, the great majority proceed to concentrate on mastering the means of life and remain indifferent to and almost oblivious of its ends. Can anyone deny the truth of Plato's words: 'The noblest of all studies is what man is and how he should

[1] *Republic*, 540.

live.' But how much time is devoted to that study by the ordinary undergraduate? This surely is educational provincialism. An ampler philosophy of education can be seen in the windows of the Chapel of King's College whose artists portrayed for their generation a vision of the history and destiny of man.

Without such a vision, conceived in the terms of the twentieth century, men are unequipped to deal with the most urgent problems of politics and civilisation, because they view them only in the light of their specialisms, and these circumscribe their view. They suffer from the fallacy, more disastrous in practice even than in reasoning, of *ignoratio elenchi*. Our political thought, for instance, is admirable so far as it goes: but it approaches its task from a narrowly intellectual angle, as though only adequate knowledge and exact thought were needed. Unfortunately, the problem is also, and predominantly, moral and spiritual. States collapse, schemes fail for many reasons: but the commonest and most fatal cause is the weakness of human character. I should be ashamed to utter such a truism if modern political thought did not habitually build its imposing palaces without foundations and ignore the cause of their brief duration and calamitous fate. That error reflects the weakness of an education preoccupied with knowledge, with the intellectual aspect, to the exclusion of any other. To concentrate on economics or political machinery or natural science is to ignore at least half the difficulties that must be overcome.

This narrowness of view is not in the great tradition of

political thought. We do not find it in Burke who wrote that 'political reason is a computing principle: adding, subtracting, multiplying and dividing, morally and not metaphysically or mathematically, true moral denominations', and who traced 'our manners, our civilisation, and all the good things which are connnected with manners and civilisation' to 'two principles—the spirit of a gentleman and the spirit of religion'. We do not find it in Hobbes, who starts from human nature and man's morals—or his lack of them. Least of all do we find it in Plato or even in Aristotle. Both of them were interested in political machinery; half of the *Laws* and most of the *Politics* are devoted to it; but whereas to us the political problem seems only a matter of Beveridge Plans, Federal Unions, Monetary Policy, and Trade Agreements, Plato and Aristotle knew that it led at once to ethics. That is one reason why they are incomparable introductions to politics: they approach it in the right spirit. So when they write a treatise on politics, education has a place in it; in the *Republic* it has the central place; and it is education conceived in a particular sense. Plato saw that the fate of any political scheme depended on the character of those who worked it, that characters were not born but made, and that they are made through education; but only through an education which leads up to the vision that he called the Idea of the Good and which is never far from it.

May not the lack of any modern counterpart to such a vision explain the restricted influence of universities on the age? In one sense, of course, their influence is obvious and immense. In their capacity of discoverers and organisers of knowledge they have brought our civilisation into being and it cannot exist without them. But having given birth to it, they desert their child. Its gravest problem is moral, spiritual; and what effect has the university on the spiritual and moral life of the world, or even on its political life so far as this is determined by spiritual and moral forces? It was not always so. Witness the originating and controlling influence of the University of Paris in the thirteenth and early fourteenth centuries; of Oxford and still more of Cambridge in preparing the Reformation in this country; in a later day, of Fichte and others in early nineteenth-century Germany. In the last twenty years two new conceptions of life have changed the course of the world—Communism and Nazism. The universities have not created or moulded them; like mercenaries, they have served the rulers of the day in Russia, Germany, Italy, supplied them with the weapons they needed and asked no questions. Outside the countries which accepted these philosophies, the universities have provided no alternative philosophy to counteract them. We have the spectacle of the democratic peoples, clinging to the traditions and memories of a nobler view of life and fighting heroically for values which they dimly discern but cannot formulate into a clear rational ideal. The universities do not help them. If it is too much to expect the universities to formulate such an ideal, they might at least have sent out men who would have done it, given the guidance for which the world is looking, and led it not only in economics and sociology, in physics and chemistry, but in even more important things. They have not done so. They do not regard spiritual ideals, except the ideal of knowledge, as their business; ultimate ends are not their concern; they provide the tools of civilisation but give no guidance for their use. What Plato calls 'the knowledge of good and evil' is almost omitted from the education which they give, and is omitted more and more, as we tend to suppose that economics and sociology give the only training needed by administrators and statesmen.

If you ask, What do you want? I make three modest suggestions as a preliminary to progress.

The first step towards curing disease is knowledge of the meaning of health: the first step to good education is a clear view of what human beings should be. We can then ask what training will produce such a type, what elements in our system serve that purpose, what changes are necessary to achieve it. In fact, we want a comprehensive, fundamental philosophy of education. (Or is our theory adequate, but forgotten in our practice?) In our quest for such a philosophy, we might start by adapting a phrase of Aristotle, and say that 'Education exists for the sake of a good life, and not only for the sake of life'. These words, with characteristic Greek sanity, recognise the dualism in human existence, its spiritual and material elements, and place them in their right order. Here is the double root from which the tree of education should grow. 'Life', livelihood, the machine, make their demands heard and we are not likely to be deaf to them or in much doubt about them. 'The good life' is more easily overlooked.

That brings me to my second suggestion. We should be less likely to overlook the problem of the good life if there were more encouragement to think seriously about it. It is, as I said earlier, extraordinary that anyone should go through a university without some study of religion or moral philosophy. These are the subjects which raise the problem of the good life and contain the answers that have been given to it. They should be an integral part of university education, and it should be impossible to get a degree without some study (but not examination) in them. Otherwise some products of our education may be like persons, who only use a certain set of muscles in their work, and in consequence are powerfully developed in one direction but deformed in others. It may be my own prejudice, but I should like to see every educated person read a book which the late Professor Cornford recently edited in a translation, with notes for English readers, that is not likely to be bettered. Plato's *Republic* is not only the greatest prose work in the secular literature of Europe, perhaps of the world, but it is also an admirable introduction to the eternal questions. It treats the state not as a political machine but as the embodiment and vehicle of the good life and therefore sees politics in relation to religion and morals. The *Republic* was composed in the Academy, but no book could be less academic, for it was written under the pressure of the problem which we have to solve, and Glaucon and Adeimantus, who open the discussion by telling Socrates that they would like to believe in goodness but find it difficult, are contemporaries of our own.

My third suggestion is that in all teaching we should pay as much attention to values as to facts. It is not enough to get people into a lecture-room and point to a dead figure labelled religion, philosophy, history, or whatever it may be. They need to see not a corpse, however well-dissected, but a living thing. The main difference between Plato's conception of education and our own is that his concern was to impart values, ours is to impart knowledge and teach people to think. In consequence, so far as we achieve our aim, we have a society strong in these directions, but vague and unstable in other values and certain to become still more so, if the influence of Christianity and of Hellenism—the only sources of values in Western civilisation—grows less in national life. Human progress depends on a double advance—increase in knowledge and the discovery of higher values. We concentrate mainly on the first, but the second is far more important. Increase of knowledge may lead to nothing but elaborate barbarism; as indeed our own age shows. The applied science and technology of which we are always demanding more will give us comfort and even luxury, but if we want a great civilisation we must look elsewhere. The ultimate importance of any nation is estimated not by its conquests, commerce or comfort but by the values which it has brought into the world and the degree to which they are embodied in its life. Take any people of the past, the Jews, the Greeks, the Romans:

what matters in their history is essentially a progress to higher values: it is by this standard that we judge them and, when our time comes, that we shall be judged. These values, of which goodness, truth and beauty are the chief, are transcendental, yet immanent in ordinary existence; far above man, yet within his reach. They inspire devotion, faith, and a self-sacrifice which is often inconsistent with common-sense, and, apart from mere animal energy, they are the only sources of intellectual and moral drive. Religion, poetry and art reveal them and keep a sense of them alive in the world. They are intangible and invisible, and we can deny their existence, for it can only be inferred from the fact that without them the spirit sickens and dies. Indeed, we may call them the vitamins of spiritual life. There are different kinds of them, present in different proportions in different subjects, so that the spirit, like the body, needs a balanced diet for perfect health. In science, the dominant vitamin is truth; in history, goodness and truth; in literature, beauty and goodness; in art, beauty. Neither history nor literature nor art have any significance apart from their values; and without them science degenerates into a meaningless materialism. Like vitamins, they can be destroyed. Science and sociology, even literature and history, can be reduced to bulk foods, destitute of any higher nutritive quality; and the destruction of vitamins is far commoner in places of education than in kitchens. It is possible to teach or treat of any subject, and ignore its values or fail to bring them out. From some lectures on Plato one might suppose that the chief interest of the *Republic* lay in the Divided Line or in the relation of the Ideas to Particulars.

Let me give instances of writers in the field of politics who do not ignore values. An interesting example is Plato's treatment of law. His *Laws* contain plain, matter-of-fact legislative enactments; but he prefaces them with so-called 'preambles', that state the spiritual principles which the laws embody, the view of life from which they spring, their values: divorced from these law is a mere routine of conduct, infused with them it becomes a living thing. In the *Laws* a whole is analysed into its constituent parts, and the value and the fact are seen separately; but commonly, and naturally, the two are fused. Aristotle's *Politics*, for instance, are founded on the scientific study of 158 constitutions; but circulating through dry detail and practical precept is something more—a sense of the values for which states exist. If Plato and Aristotle are too remote, I should give a great Cambridge historian as an example of a modern teacher who emphasised values. It is not merely the vast learning that makes Lord Acton's historical writing impressive; it is not his style, which was ordinary; it is his power of making the reader see history as a struggle of great forces of good and evil, wisdom and folly, justice and iniquity, the free and the unfree mind. History—and other subjects—should, I suggest, be taught in the spirit of Acton rather than of Bury.

It may be objected that insistence on values will sacrifice truth to edification and convert study into preaching. No one could bring either of these charges against Aristotle, and Acton's insistence that the historian should pass moral judgments was certainly not inconsistent with devotion to truth or to research. After all, to betray truth is to ignore one of the greatest values, and in any case values do not alter facts. The facts about Frederick the Great and Bismarck are not changed by any moral judgment on them, and the evil in their lives can be condemned without denying their genius. As for sermonizing, a sense of values is perhaps best imparted by those who feel them intensely but never mention them; as a good actor does not pause to comment on the agony of Lear or the jealousy of Othello, but simply conveys it. But, whatever means are used, it is essential that a sense of these values on which civilisation depends for its quality should be imparted and that no one should study a subject without becoming conscious of something great, something momentous in it. The small rock-pools of the seashore have a life and beauty and interest of their own, but they owe their freshness and purity to the tides of a vast ocean far beyond our sight and ken.

There are many values. Will they lead to the pursuit of divergent goods and become in turn sources of confusion, or can they be brought under a single principle and create the harmony of a complete human life? Plato thought to find their unity in a vision of Goodness which embraced and co-ordinated all other goods. Others wish to trace values back to a material origin and explain them on purely naturalistic grounds. To their efforts we may perhaps apply Plato's remarks on the rationalisers of myths and say that it is work for an ingenious, laborious and not very fortunate man:[1] if it succeeded, values would lose their compelling power. I would rather think of them as Sophocles thought of the moral laws:

οὐρανίαν
δι' αἰθέρα τεκνωθέντες, ὧν Ὄλυμπος
πατὴρ μόνος, οὐδέ νιν
θνατὰ φύσις ἀνέρων
ἔτικτεν, οὐδέ μή ποτε λάθα κατακοιμάσῃ,
μέγας ἐν τούτοις θεός, οὐδὲ γηράσκει.

'They were born where Heaven is.
Mortal parent have they none,
Nor shall man's forgetfulness ever make them sleep.
A god in them is great. He grows not old.'[2]

And I believe that they find their unity and explanation in that philosophy of life which, starting in Greece, and enriched and fulfilled by Christianity, has been the creative and formative force in Western civilisation.

[1] *Phaedrus*, 229.
[2] Sophocles, *O.T.* 865 f. (tr. Sheppard).